FOUR STEPS TO BUSINESS PLANNING FOR PLAN-PHOBIC CREATIVES

FOUR STEPS TO
BUSINESS PLANNING FOR
PLAN-PHOBIC
CREATIVES

Goose Your Muse Tips for Creatives Series

Y J Kohano

K
E

Nanokas Press

A Division of Kochanowski Enterprises

FOUR STEPS TO BUSINESS PLANNING FOR PLAN-PHOBIC CREATIVES
Goose Your Muse Tips for Creatives Series

Nanokas Press/KE Press books may be ordered through booksellers or by contacting:

Kochanowski Enterprises/Nanokas Press
PO Box 1274
Clackamas, OR 97015-9594
www.yvonnekohano.com
yvonne@yvonnekohano.com

Cover design: John Kochanowski

ISBN:
978-1-940738-12-3 (e)
978-1-940738-13-0 (sc)

Nanokas Press First Edition: 09-06-2016

Contents

FOUR STEPS TO BUSINESS PLANNING FOR PLAN-PHOBIC CREATIVES

WHY YOU NEED THIS BOOK

I know, I know. I've heard it many times. Planning makes you nervous. You feel it inhibits your creative sensibilities. You create when and what the muse tells you to, not to meet a preset plan. Planning takes up too much time. Besides, what would you put in a plan? *You are con-plan-phobic!* In other words, you really *hate* planning.

Or you're at the other end of continuum. You absolutely *love* to plan. Your to-do list is your bible, and you study it every day. Checking things off that list is an obsession. Give you color-coding with a detailed filing system and you are over the proverbial moon. *You are pro-plan-phobic!* You would happily spend hours in a day on planning.

Or you're in the middle, that place where you know you *should* plan, but you're not sure *why*. People tell you it's important to guide your creative life, but, like our friends in no-plan land, you wouldn't know where to start. *You are mid-plan-phobic!*

```
┌──────────────────────────────────────────────────────────────┐
│   Con-Plan-Phobic                          Pro-Plan-Phobic     │
│   ←-------------------------A---------------------------B----------------→     │
│        Planning is Scary!              Planning is Fun!        │
│                                                                │
│     Are you more toward the A end or the B?  No wrong answer!  │
└──────────────────────────────────────────────────────────────┘
```

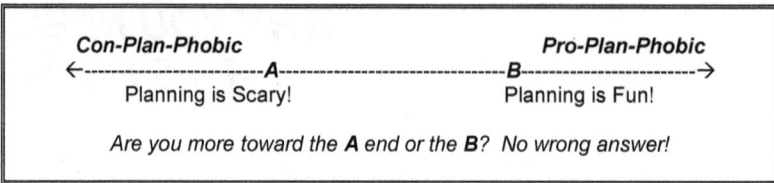

No matter where you fall on the continuum of desire in planning for your creative life, you can make things easier, simpler, and faster by designing the _right kind_ of business plan. I'm not talking about the whole mission-vision-values-goals-objectives-tactics and documentation that would make even the most organized person's head spin. We want things focused, direct and supportive. ***FOUR STEPS TO BUSINESS PLANNING FOR THE PLAN-PHOBIC CREATIVE*** gives you a useful tool to guide your best creative life.

Still not sure this kind of planning can help grow your creative life? Flip through the next few pages and see what resonates with YOU!

BEING A CREATIVE COMES WITH BAGGAGE

Our creative lives are dynamic. Whether we create through photos, music, physical art or the written word, the flow – *that moment of complete absorption in the work we're creating* – is what we seek. You know that old saying, that you can have two out of three, price, quality or convenience? That applies here too. Creativity doesn't happen without three things – **_time_**, **_inspiration_**, and **_skills_** – and you only get to pick two of these!

Here's an example. I am a writer. Some days, I sit down to create new words and I stare at that blinking cursor, empty of inspiration and ideas. All of my tools surround me, and yet – nothing happens. I've primed the pump in every way I know how (including caffeine) but...

Let's be obvious – a writer needs to write! So I write. I might end up deleting every word, but in most cases, using that time means something will be salvageable. I have applied two out of the three – I had the time, and I applied skills. But *inspiration*? Not happening.

My painter friend has loads of inspiration. She looks at a scene and thinks of six different ways to represent it, either

in different painting mediums (like oils or watercolors) or even outside of her box in a textile form. She is a font of new ideas. However, she's also a busy mom with a stack of responsibilities, so she never has as much time to devote to her art as she'd like. Inspiration – check. Skills – oh yes indeed. But no *time*.

What does this have to do with planning? Everything! If you have a plan for your creative life, you know how to create time in your calendar. When you have that time, you are prepared to use it wisely because you have invested in your craft (part of your plan) to develop your skills. And you have inspiration, because you have a stack of upcoming ideas to choose from. Oh yes, that's in the plan too!

REASONS TO PLAN

Here are a few reasons why we should plan:

- To name and then remove <u>challenges</u>

- To set <u>priorities</u>

- To guide <u>decisions</u>

- To <u>focus</u> our productive hours

- To direct our <u>growth</u>

- To create <u>targets</u>

- To avoid <u>overwhelm</u>

Let's examine each one more closely.

> *Creatives love to splash in the puddles of the unknown.*

Challenges

Creativity happens at the intersection of mistakes and reality. In other words, it's a happy accident! I don't know about your creative life, but in mine, *I'd love to have happy accidents all the time.* All it takes is a little planning.

Our creative reality is that we will never have enough time, inspiration or skills to do everything we want to do. When we're starting out, we might not yet know what we *don't know* in terms of our craft. For example, a chef might be great at combining flavors but not yet know various cooking techniques that can optimize those when brought together. A beginning photographer might have a terrific eye, but does not yet understand the settings on the camera to optimize the image.

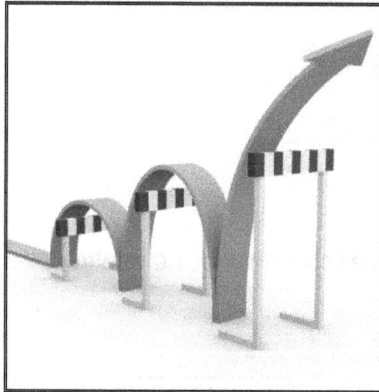

Skills are hurdles, something most of us continue to learn to jump in our creative lives. The more we know, the better we understand that we've only scratched the surface. There is always more to learn and new trends or techniques to analyze for our use. But can we plan to grow? Absolutely! Your plan might include professional development, repetition and practice, or exploration of new avenues. In other words, **you plan to remove the challenge of not knowing by planning to learn more**.

Available time is a major challenge for creatives. As many of my writing friends say, planting your butt in the chair is the only way to get it done. I know of no published authors who create *only* when all of the stars align down to the smallest molecule. Writers, yes, but they are not published. Creatives make time for their craft, even if it's only minutes a day. They plan for it – more on this in a few.

You might be scratching your head right now. You understand the benefits of planning for time and skills, but how do you plan for inspiration? Many creatives think of inspiration as a spontaneous force, a whim of the muse so to speak. I don't know which of my characters will choose to talk to me on a certain day, but I can plan time to feed the muse so that when I'm poised at the keyboard, she is too.

Priorities

Most of us think planning's primary benefit is in helping to set goals, and because we have goals, to better understand our priorities. That is true, and it is also true that planning allows us to better grasp what we need to do ourselves versus what we need to pay others to do for us.

As a self-published author, I am at the helm of a (mini) publishing empire. I set priorities for time, inspiration and skills (our happy threesome). I also empty the wastebaskets and order the printer ink, but those are priorities too.

For creatives, planning our priorities allows us to make the most of our most cherished resource, time. For example,

as I write this, I have a national writers conference I am attending in three days, and a book festival where I'm exhibiting and selling the fruits of my labors in three weeks. And a long to-do list to accomplish with tight deadlines. Add in alterations to a family schedule that should have been fixed, and I was left with small pockets of time to juggle my many tasks.

But since I have a plan, I know what priorities are most important, and I know approximately how much time I need to allot to them. A "found" fifteen minutes turns into a completed task that would otherwise drag me away from writing time. I didn't have to think about it – I just did it. Planning lets us set priorities and takes the hassle out of thinking "what's next?" More on this in Step 4.

Decisions

Hand in hand with priorities, planning allows us to make the most of our decision points as creatives. A musician knows that recording a new song will require decisions about the instruments used, voices singing back-up, and style of sound effects, for example. Knowing all of that may not be important in the moment, but it will be in the future.

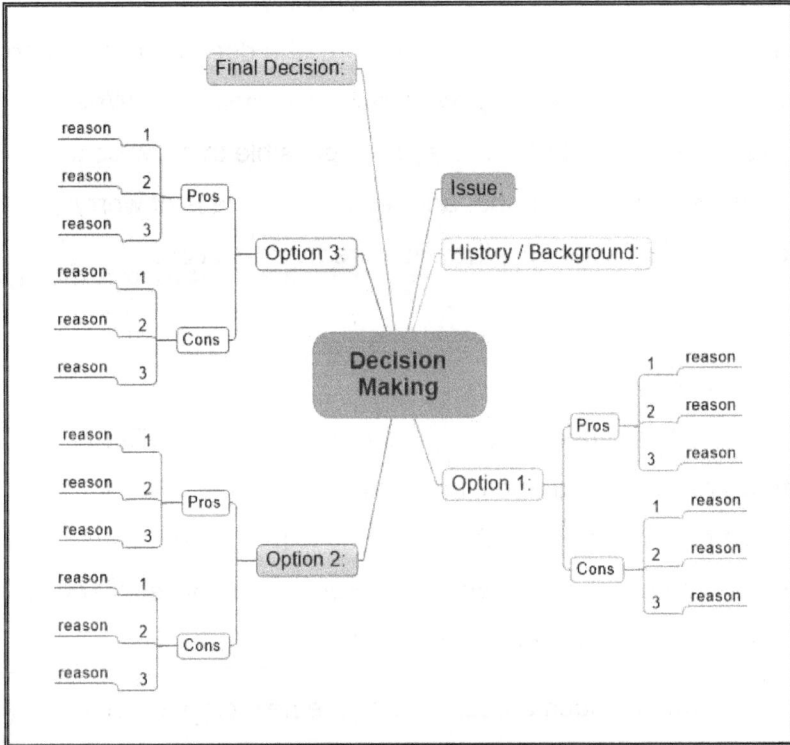

Understanding <u>what</u> allows us to let go of stress that we might miss a step. Understanding <u>when</u> we need to know allows us the freedom to set it out of our minds (i.e., stop worrying about it) until the decision is necessary. Forethought and planning will also give us time (there it is again) to gather more data to inform the decision. Not sure if that artsy photo scene will best be captured at dawn or dusk? You have time to research it if you already have a plan for the photo shoot.

Before you throw your hands up and declare there is no way you would know all of the decisions you will need to make before you get to the point, breathe deeply. There is no way. *Creativity is a happy accident*, remember? We want to set up the most effective system possible to allow us to be creative when we can be, and reduce the stress of worrying about other things until they have reached fruition.

Focus

Yup, still beating that productive time thing. This, though, may be our most important sense of time, and that is focusing on time to create. Planning is my friend, though, and if I know what I need to work on (projects, deadlines, shows), I can make the most of my creative time.

I am as much a free spirit as the next creative, but I am also practical and rational. I know it is too easy for me to be busy but NOT productive. Creatives love to splash in the puddles of the unknown, but if we do so and find ourselves then wandering the path of work not completed, it creates stress. I don't know about you, but stress is a real creativity killer for me! We want to remove the stress so we can concentrate on the creative part. (Yes, I know some of us need stress to meet deadlines, but that's the subject for a standalone book!)

Many creative gurus will tell you that you should plan for segments of creative time. It could be before or after your day job. It could be your day job itself. Whether you write appointments with yourself in a planner to be creative, or you commit to using part of a lunch hour, a period after the kids go to bed, or early hours after setting back the alarm clock, making time means planning for time.

More than setting the time aside, though, you have to understand what you're going to do with it. If an hour of painting time means all you get a chance to do is prepare your palette, is that the best use of your time? Would you be better off finding a means to mark off more time, or working on a different project? Part of this comes from understanding how we work, and understanding that our methods evolve over time too. Making the most of our productive time comes from our next point, growth.

Growth

I look back with a certain yearning fondness to my early days of fiction writing. I would rise in the morning and write for hours, uninhibited by thoughts about release dates, deadlines to send manuscripts to editors or advanced readers, and the business side of running my little empire. I simply created. Sometimes, I miss those days.

But then again, I have to set aside the rationalizing smoke-and-mirrors to be honest. I know more now, which means I can provide a better product. Knowing more means taking a good look at my skills on an ongoing basis and deciding where I need to grow. I plan for it, whether it is in the form of attending an educational seminar or inviting critiques from trusted creative friends. Creativity is dynamic, and as our skill grows, what we need to do next changes too.

Why bring this up? Sometimes growth doesn't arrive in the ways we believe that it would. Growth is a series of building blocks, things we either follow in an order or set on top of each other to roam higher. There is no "one way". An apprentice might not become a master in the same modes and methods as the teacher. Planning for growth leads us to new opportunities, and having a plan means we know if those fit within our big picture.

Targets

No, these are not necessarily goals, though it might be helpful to think about them that way if you are used to business jargon. Targets are static in the otherwise dynamic plan of our paths. There are many paths and methods to get there, as long as we know where 'there' is. By way of example, here are the targets for production of this book. I use a spreadsheet, but checklists work just as well.

Production Schedule	7/30	8/6	8/13	8/20	8/27	9/3	9/10	9/17	9/24
GYM2 - Planning									
First edit			█						
Second edit			█						
Beta edit			█						
Final read/changes				█					
Book description & key words				█					
Assign ISBNs				█					
Front & back matter				█					
Format for ebook				█					
Final cover thumbnail changes				█					
Upload to Kindle					█				
Print cover production					█				
Format for print					█				
Upload to CreateSpace					█				
Verify print copy						█			
Verify Bowker						█			
Order books							█		
Upload to Kobo							█		
Upload to IngramSparks							█		
Apply for copyright							█		
Link FCs/Amazon author page							█		

Targets can take many forms. Common examples are financial baselines (support myself with my craft), events (show or deadline), items (a book, record, or menu), external validation (an award win), and self-actualization (to know I can do it). Whatever it is, though, there will be a number of ways to reach it. Just as a destination can follow many roads, the path the arrow takes to the target varies based on atmospheric conditions and equipment. (And skill...)

Defining (another word for planning) those targets allows us to plan the possible ways to reach them. Maybe you are writing fiction, and you want to support your family by doing it. That takes time since the chance of hitting it big on your first attempt is up there with being struck by lightning. In the meantime, you might spend part of your magic trio (time, inspiration, skills) selling nonfiction articles to blogs, enewsletters and magazines, until you have enough inventory of released titles to make a regular income stream of royalties possible. The clerk at the grocery store doesn't care if I'm spending my royalties or contracted fees – money's money.

Overwhelm

I hear this a lot from creative people.

"But I don't know where to start!"

Understood. You risk being submerged by that big wave, overwhelm.

Answer: You begin at the beginning.

Well duh. It's easy to say but harder to put into practice. I mentioned my conference and book show. In order to have the books to sell at the show, I needed to order them. To order them, I had to publish them. To publish them, I had to polish them. You see where this is going.

I fell into the well of overwhelm, and I wasn't sure how to crawl back out. Planning saved my sanity – and my (yes) time. Rather than spend my time wringing my hands over how I was going to get it done, I made a plan, and then I executed it. Mine is on that electronic spreadsheet I showed you earlier. Yours may be all in your head. (Bravo! My brain needs it written down.) Regardless, *having a plan* reduces the worrying.

Overwhelm doesn't have to be a negative, either. Ever heard the phrase 'having too many choices'? That, like having a surplus of great ideas, can cause you to do nothing, because you can't decide what to do. You have the time and the skills, plus more inspiration than you know how to handle. **Planning, that's the answer!**

Let's face it, being a creative is not easy. We have to find ways to stay motivated when faced with life's usual and customary challenges. We need cheerleaders in our lives to help encourage us when we cannot encourage ourselves. We need to embrace change because it's a fact of human existence. We need to understand trends in our chosen field to remain supple and flexible. To handle any and all of these, we need a plan.

Planning does not need to take a major time investment, nor do you need to make it as detailed as the fine strokes of a gnat's eyelash. For you **con-plan-phobics**, a plan is important so that you can spend your time doing what you love – being creative – and not trying to answer the panicked question of what comes next. For the **pro-plan-phobics**, simplifying your plan gives you permission to create more, rather than spending your creative time planning. And for the **mid-plan-phobic**, this book will guide you to the things you need to know without becoming muddled in the things that are not going to keep you creating.

Ready to dig into the hard stuff? Let's start planning!

STEP 1 - WHAT'S MY PURPOSE?

What are we as creatives?

In general terms, we are:

- Experience junkies

- Extraverts for inspiration

- Introverts for production

- Beauty- and truth-seekers

- Agreeable, except when someone interrupts our art

- Neurotic about being creative

Does this sound like you? That last two points in particular resonate with me. If I'm not writing, I get crabby! And don't bother me when I'm in the zone!

Even as we understand the general traits, each of us is different in the amplification and origin of our creative power. For example, if you are someone who researches extensively before you create, no matter what the subject or medium, you might be crazed with the need to understand how much you know, how much more there is to learn, and how you can fill in the gaps. Others may find that stifles them.

It is important, however, to recognize we have a lot to give. We're in the business of creating art, beauty and entertainment. It exists across multiple formats, and it pleases diverse audiences. This is not a narrow band, but a broad one. What's your niche on that band? More importantly, how will you define yourself to appeal to what might be very different message receivers in your audience?

Purpose is personal. There are no right or wrong answers. Size does not matter, nor does intensity. We are open to experience, because we seek beauty and truth in the messiness of creativity. Beauty and truth are in the eye of the beholder, remember, so what I see and what you see may not agree.

And that's okay. Don't rush it. This is big picture stuff. We will work on the details later. Your wants, your desires, are what you should be focused on now. Let's dig deeper into personal creative purpose.

A side note: The forms represented in these steps appear as a set at the end of this book. They are also available in an editable text document at my website, www.GooseYourMuse.com. The blank form for each specific section appears at the end of the topic.

> *If we aren't happy with our lives, what's the point?*

WHAT DO I WANT?

Answer the following question:

In my best creative life, I want...

This is about **WANT**, which may be different from being realistic! It may take a considerable amount of time to satisfy this want. If you don't know what you want, how will you be satisfied with your creative life? How will you know when you get 'there', wherever there might be?

Some of us may feel a trace of guilt about stating what we want. Here it is, permission. It's okay to want fame and fortune. We all need to eat and keep a roof over our heads. Recognition from the outside work is validating too. But in the end, if we aren't happy with our lives, what's the point?

You may want to snap at me right now, telling me it's not that simple. You have responsibilities and others who rely on you. Me too, but there are many ways to keep the coffers full, ways that aren't as personally taxing and requiring the same level of commitment as being creative. Being creative is HARD WORK!

My thinking on this has evolved over the years. While my *formal* fiction author career only dates back to 2011, I've been a creative since I came out of the womb. As a child, my parents gave my sister and me used cardboard boxes and old sheets and encouraged us to play make believe. I have had creative jobs – management consultant, professor, photographer, writer. I have been telling stories and helping people to understand the world through those stories for as long as I've been able to talk.

And I like money as much as the next person, not for the dollars *per se*, but for the experiences they can offer me. Experience junkie, from the top of my graying head to the worn soles of my feet. I have a natural curiosity about how things work. My first word was not 'Ma' or 'Da', but '**why**'. But even as an experience junkie, that would not be enough to keep me going when the words aren't coming, the plot is now in a tangle, and the release deadline looms.

I answer the big picture question like this: ***In my best creative life, I want to give my audience an engaging escape from their daily lives.***

Okay, your turn!

In my best creative life, I want...

> *If we had more beauty through the arts, we might have less bloodshed in the world.*

WHY DO I WANT THIS?

Let's repeat an important fact. Being creative is hard work. Plenty of times, you'll want to quit. When those times come, reminding yourself about why you want to be creative might be the only thing to pull you through the darkness into the sunlight on the other side. Formulate an answer to this question:

I want to be a creative because...

There are no wrong answers here, and no one will think the worse of you if you select option D instead of A. No one will know – except you. Honesty time! And what you'll probably find is that your reasons are a mix of many of these. If you find it difficult or confusing to figure out why you want to be creative, here are some common reasons.

Art

I want to create because I can add beauty to the world. The work I create will be unlike anyone else's in the world (always true) and the world needs more of what I have to offer (also always true). My unique contribution, even if it is never seen by another person, will be enough. If you are pursuing the creative life for outside recognition, this means surviving the disappointments when you do not win the award, get selected for the show, or have your work picked up by the mainstream.

You might have heard this already, though. Does the world need more XXX? No matter what you're creating, I believe the answer should be a shouted YES! If we had more beauty through the arts, we might have less bloodshed. Stepping down from the soapbox now…

> *Don't settle until you're satisfied you've done your best, the very best you can do right now.*

Passion

Creating has always been your dream. You always wanted to paint a picture or craft a song or write your memoires. You do this not because you're particularly good at it or you think it will become the new top-of-the-charts. You do it because it's fun! A good friend of mine decided to take up gourd-painting a few years after he retired. He'd never been artsy, not in the least. But he thought it looked like fun. And now, after a couple of years doing it, he's advanced to carving and burning and other sophisticated techniques, and his work could easily be salable.

Never allow yourself to lose that sense of enjoyment, of passion in your creativity. How many times have you thought this about someone well-known in your craft? One day, you see their current work and you wonder, gee, where did the exciting things they used to create go? Their results have become stale, boring and same-old-same-old because they are now creating not from passion, but churning to feed the market. When passion is lost, it can be obvious in what we produce. My gourd-driven friend says he might get a table at a craft show, but he's not turning his passion into a business. That would take all of the fun out of it!

Money

There is nothing wrong with creating for money. I know of no creative endeavor, except perhaps warbling with your voice alone, that does not require some kind of investment. Painters buy paint. Musicians buy instruments and often electronics. Writers need professional editors. We all have to buy something to feed our creative production line, and few of us can afford to create without recouping some part of our investment.

Financial reward alone won't be enough to power you through the painful times, though. There will be days when being the front door greeter at a big box store will seem like it pays better than your craft, even if you work at your craft full time!

In reality, most creative fields have a very small slice of top-tier financial successes. On the other hand, maybe as many as eighty-percent of the substantial contributors in the field will be what's called mid-listers. They don't make enough to buy fancy homes in multiple cities or hire a full staff, but they pay the bills and have a loyal following. Aim to be one of them instead of being struck by lightning! Your chances of success are much more likely!

Lifestyle

Being an artist as a full time endeavor is a lifestyle choice. You are your own boss. Even if you have contracts for the production and distribution of your work, you create first for yourself. You need to feel the end result is acceptable, even if it's not reaching that mythical point of perfection. (Creatives always want to be perfect, but by definition, that does not exist for more than a nanosecond!)

Choosing to be a full-time creative as your line of work, or even as a part time gig, can give you an incredible sense of freedom. You are free to express yourself in whichever way satisfies you. And with that, you also have responsibilities. Even as a self-published author, I have external deadlines, expectations of others (readers) to meet, and both of those inside myself too. Most of us (and I'm guessing you fall into this category too) are harder on ourselves than anyone else can be on us. Freedom is the offset to that responsibility.

> *You have to know how you will continue to support yourself, both from a security perspective and inside your creative head.*

Career

Career is different from lifestyle as a motivating factor. As an example, some people love to create music as a component of their lifestyle, but they would not want to be a musician for their professional career. Usually, that's because one of the other motivating factors noted above is more important to them, and they don't see that possibility being met based on their skills or choices.

If you pick being a creative full-time as your career, please make sure you put a safety net under that high wire! Before you make that commitment, learn everything you can about what the career entails. Even the best creative among us has bad runs, and when those occur, you have to know how you will continue to support yourself, both from a security perspective and *inside your creative head.* The people who hit it big the first time out are the one-percent of the one-percenters. They are not the norm.

Now that you've thought about the 'why' question, capture what you've learned. Some people like to make a pie chart and cut it into pieces based on how important each slice is to them. Others like to make a pyramid with the biggest motivator on the bottom, the foundation of it all. Or make a list. Don't make this a big deal, like writing out your rationale about your selections, unless it helps you come to an understanding. This is YOUR plan – make this a snapshot YOU understand.

Here's a tip – I find it helpful to think about my reasons why in terms of winning the lottery. If I won a big prize and never had to worry about money again, what would I choose to do with my creative life? I'll always write – though maybe not producing books quite as fast! What's your choice?

I want to be a creative because...	
Important Factors:	
Art	
Passion	
Money	
Lifestyle	
Career	
Other	

> *In the flow to the exclusion of all else means being creative is the only thing you're working on.*

WHAT DO I VALUE?

Hey, this is NOT the beginning of mission-vision-values! This is about setting personal guidelines to give you direction when you have to make choices. Everything comes with a trade-off, and doing one thing means you can't do another. (Unless you've been able to clone yourself. If the answer to that is yes, please email me immediately! I want what you have!)

And before anyone brings up multi-tasking as a way to do more as a creative, I'll present my bias. If you're in the flow of being creative, you're using up all of your intellectual and emotional bandwidth being creative. Being in the zone is a vacuum that sucks out everything else. How many times have you known someone to be creating and they don't even hear the world around them or notice something major happening? In the flow to the exclusion of all else means it's the only thing you're working on.

Time to think about the values that drive your creative life. These are the <u>good</u> boundaries, the things marking your journey, not challenges that keep you from moving forward. Here are some broad categories to consider.

Belief Systems

The most common boundary creatives set relates to our belief systems. For example, an author might only want to write sweet inspirational romances. Another writer might be committed to avoiding curse words, even in thriller/suspense stories. Someone else might not want to write anything erotic.

The examples don't end with writers. A chef can be equally committed to farm-to-table or vegetarianism. A musician's focus could be on instrumentals, or on classic rock, or on ballads. The same applies to gardeners using only native plants in their design or sculptors only using stone or wood.

You will notice that many of these variations sound like categorization, and that is true. We categorize our creative work (genre or style) as a shorthand to help others understand what we're working on. However, if we're not careful, it can also be a way to limit ourselves. If that is a conscious decision, no problem, as long as you have made the choice.

> *Seek satisfaction instead of the unachievable,*
> *perfection.*

Satisfaction First

Does this sound like you? "If I can't produce a perfect product, I'm wasting my time."

Practice, anyone?

The common belief is that it takes 10,000 hours to get "good" at something. Assuming you only have time to be creative around your day job and your family, this means some years will pass between beginning and "good". Patience is required! As a whole, we humans aren't very patient with ourselves.

I know many writers, for example, who attempt to get the first draft "right", as in perfect. It slows them down. They are so busy trying to perfect the words in a sentence, they forgot about the rest of the paragraph. Furthermore, by the time they're ready to move on, they forgot the flow of what they were writing.

Research on creative types tells us that we produce some of our very best work while we're in the flow of it. It consumes us, blocking out the rest of the world. Nothing and no one exists in that moment but the work in front of us. I love that feeling!

I've also learned to harness it. I write a draft very quickly, throwing words at the page like so many raindrops in a downpour while I am in the flow. I still want the end result to be as close to perfection as possible, but that can wait for the editing process.

> *Compare yourself to <u>no one</u> with the intent of finding yourself lacking.*

Internal Struggles

Doubts besiege us as creatives. How can I be *good enough*? Look at my peers and the success they have achieved. Why am I still lagging behind?

Time can be your friend here. Take a mental (or physical) snapshot of where you are at the beginning or any midpoint of your creative career. Down the road, when you feel those internal struggles welling up, compare the past to the present. I'm betting you'll be pleasantly surprised with what you learn about your progress!

Compare yourself to <u>no one</u> with the intent of finding yourself lacking. Look to others as exemplars, as models, as evidence that you too can succeed. It's only through recognizing these common internal struggles, learning from them, and setting them aside that we can progress as creatives.

> *Self-doubt sabotages more creative work than any other emotion.*

Internal Messaging

This could also be you. You receive compliments on your work, but you feel like a fraud. You worry that you will be discovered for the imposter you are. Your work is not as good as anyone says, and you are living with self-doubts and sabotaging your own best efforts, if you are even creating, that is.

Feeling like an imposter can block us from what we really want, so it's important to recognize when we engage in negative self-talk and change our language. Ignoring this tendency (which is held by 70% of the population according to experts) distorts our values and how we act on them. Examining messages we send ourselves and making sure they act for our best interests instead of against us will be critical to our success.

> *Where there is risk, there is also opportunity for success.*

Risk Acceptance

All of us are willing to accept different levels of risk. There are a multitude of reasons for this, including our upbringing, the way we're wired, and the strength of our safety net. For some, there will never be "enough" money to feel secure *only* as a creative. We might need to expand the concept of how we work as a creative to feel comfortable about having enough.

For example, someone who produces physical works of art like paintings or artistic photos might need to explore contract work. Can you also create graphics for advertising or print publications? Can you illustrate someone's books? Can you prepare motivational posters or corporate training documents? Even working within your medium, you can find other ways to express yourself while generating a regular income stream.

Now that you've considered some of the major values that guide our creative life, how will you answer this question?

The values that guide my creative life are...	
Important Factors:	
Belief Systems	
Satisfaction First	
Internal Struggles	
Imposter Syndrome	
Comfort with Risk	
Other	

WHAT DOES SUCCESS LOOK LIKE?

Now it's your time to wrap up the big picture and consider what you believe success looks like. Visualizing your success will you help you achieve it. Success is not an accident, at least not often.

Think about the questions at the end of each segment above. Return to them as you have new insights about your best creative life. And answer the question in the following form:

I will be satisfied in my best creative life when...

STEP 2 - WHO AM I?

This section tackles the creative "me" that exists to serve our creative process. The first step in any assessment is determining where you are today. Most of us have at some point been exposed to a self-analysis or examination of an organization we're part of. The intention is to inventory our **strengths**, **weaknesses**, **opportunities** and **threats**. This is an important exercise, because unless we are honest with ourselves about the gifts we have and those that need further development, it's almost impossible to make progress and improve our outcomes.

Strengths are those internal things we're good at, things that will help our creative life. **Opportunities** are the positive aspects of our external environment that also support more creativity. We want to leverage or maximize these internal and external benefits.

We want to reduce our **weaknesses** (internal) and **threats** (external). I like to think of this as overcoming anything that holds us back, whether it's negative self-talk or naysayers saying it to me. Recognizing these things helps us come up with a PLAN to work past them. In some cases, like external threats, we might just be able to recognize them, period, and accept that they are in our way. Don't worry –

you can get around them! Compensating actions are part of your toolbox once you recognize the externality is there.

Another method to use in thinking about these broad categories would be: **Strengths and weaknesses** are things you and I can directly **control**. **Opportunities and threats** are out of our direct control, but we **CAN control how we react** to them.

We'll move into the inventory phase of our planning process now. The following discussion is designed to get you thinking about what your assessment needs to include. A side note – I dislike using the word 'weaknesses', so you'll see the other side of 'strengths' noted as 'improvements'.

We don't yet know what we don't know.

PERSONAL INVENTORY

The obvious first consideration is your preparation for your creative life. What education, experience and skills do you have in your chosen creative field? Now think bigger. How might you past prepare you for the future you want?

How have my experiences prepared me for the creative life I want to explore? How can I improve upon what I know to do my best work?

Here are talking points to get you started. Think of each in terms of both internal strengths and areas you might need to improve.

Life Skills

When I began publishing, someone asked me if I'd always been a writer. By implication, they meant a fiction writer, a writer of stories. My first reaction was to say no. Growing up, my best friend was a fiction writer, and she was so good, I compared myself to her and found my skills lacking, so I didn't write past keeping an occasional journal.

That was the first blush. The longer I thought about this, though, the clearer I became on how my past prepared me for being a storyteller in the present. When I was a child, my parents gave us puppets. We made a theater out of a big old box. Sets were painter posters and we dressed the puppets up in costumes. We "wrote" plays and musicals.

Fast forward to career choices in adulthood. I was a management consultant, a university professor, and a public speaker. Consultants must be able to tell the story of a situation or process in order to explain the analysis to others. Sometimes these were complex ideas requiring comparisons to something the audience was familiar with in order to help them understand. Imagine making financial analysis into a game! The same was true in teaching at the graduate level.

Who are the most engaging speakers on the circuit? They are great storytellers who have us hanging on to every word.

As I came to realize, I had always been a good storyteller. I just hadn't been applying that talent in a fiction setting. Now I get to make up people, places and conflicts out of the void!

STRENGTHS: What life skills have I developed that will apply to my best creative life?

IMPROVEMENTS: What life skills do I need to add to my capabilities to be a more effective creative?

> *Be willing to practice with an eye toward constant improvement.*

Resources

Sometimes, we don't have the resources ourselves to be the kind of creative we want to be. Whether it's education or practice, we don't yet know what we don't know, which makes it hard for us to assess our skills with honesty. I'll be the first one to tell you that sometimes, ignorance is bliss! We can fool ourselves into thinking we're good at something because we know no better. On the other hand, though, what if you could make a few simple changes and change so-so good into great? We need role models and examples to expand our thinking.

There are many ways to educate ourselves. In your chosen creative field, you will undoubtedly receive advice across a spectrum. You need a degree – or you don't. You need to serve as an apprentice, or maybe not. You must have natural talent – or you can develop it.

There are only three absolutes, in my humble opinion. To make the move from good to great, you need to be willing to practice with an eye toward constant improvement. You must remain flexible and willing to change as the market for what you're selling changes. And you need to be willing to accept constructive criticism and decide how you want to act on it. Practice makes you better, as long as it's not so self-absorbed that you never think about how you can improve. Criticism of the right nature allows us to see our work more clearly than we can by ourselves.

How do you find this? Think about your resources. What books or magazines can you read on the subject? What classes can you take? Are there groups in your area or online with members who are already doing what you want to do? Can you visit the masters, as in a gallery or museum or at a reading?

STRENGTHS: What models or examples am I already utilizing in my resources?

IMPROVEMENTS: What resources can I tap into as a means to improve on the things I identified in my personal assessment? Warning: You may find more items to add to your lists as you explore the exemplars in your creative field!

> *In every criticism we feel is unfounded, there is a kernel of truth.*

Perspective

We all have it – perspective. We see things in a particular way, through the veils of our beliefs and what our experiences have taught us. Usually, however, we're better at seeing things around us than seeing them in ourselves! That's when you need a little help from your friends.

In the last chapter, you spent time developing your list of values that guide your creative career. This is where you start as you consider your perspective. Your values color the way you see your creative career.

Next, verify your self-view with trusted people around you. Ask them how *they* see you. Do they agree with your sense of self? If things differ, how do they differ, and why do they think so?

This may sound like you are being defensive and demanding evidence, but sometimes when it comes to an honest view of ourselves, that's necessary! Our friends can see our strong points – and often have no problem pointing them out to us, as their own imposter syndrome kicks in.

Likewise, there are those who love to cause us grief by sharing the negative, but this too is perspective. In my experience, in every criticism we feel is unfounded, there is a kernel of truth. Uncover that secret, and you understand more about your perspective on the world.

STRENGTHS: What do others think of how you perceive your skills and capabilities?

IMPROVEMENTS: What can you also learn from criticism?

> *The person you are influences the person you become – but it does not limit you.*

Work Habits

Now that you understanding your driving factors and have verified the list with trusted confidantes, recognition of your work habits come next. Why is this broken out as a separate section? Being a creative person differs from being, say, a factory worker or an accountant. Even if you are creating under a deadline, the energy to create comes from a vague something inside you. It isn't part of a set, repetitive process. Neither is it subject to a list of rules and regulations about how creative work should be done (no matter what some people might tell you). Being creative is living in the "IS".

Are you self-directed in completing your work without someone panting over your shoulder, or do you need to have a deadline in front of you to force you into motion? Does your project need to percolate for a while to make progress, or is the creative vision delivered whole? When you start a project, is it imperative that you work through to its completion without touching anything else, or do you have multiple works in progress? Do you plan every step in the creative process, or do you jump in and trust inspiration will come to you as you need it?

These questions represent the opposite ends of creative continuums. Chances are you are blend in each of these areas, though you will tend toward one end or the other. There is no correct place to be. Instead, recognizing how you work is an asset. Once you know this, you can leverage your favorite processes in your creative life. Need more time to formulate your vision? Plan for that time? Better under deadlines? How can you set reasonable but frequent little steps to meet?

Another component of work habits reflects the way you do business. Are you organized, or does the mere idea of a filing system give you the heebie-jeebies? Are you easily distracted by bright shiny things, or can you stay on task? How well can you manage the stress of running your creative business? These capabilities are things you can improve upon – as long as you recognize what they are.

STRENGTHS: What beneficial work habits do you have for your creative life?

IMPROVEMENTS: How will you plan to take advantage of the way you work rather than fight against it?

Ready to pull this section together? Here's that handy form!

Personal Inventory

How have my experiences prepared me for the creative life I want to explore?		
	STRENGTHS	IMPROVEMENTS
Life Skills		
Resources		
Perspective		
Work Habits		
Other		

CRAFT ANALYSIS

Now that you understand what you as a person bring to the creative table, you assess the level of your skills in your chosen creative field. This might be uncomfortable for some of us, and there's a good reason. We're human, and we tend to either over-estimate our abilities, or under-estimate them. No clue why we can't hit them spot on!

What am I good at, and how well do I know my craft?

> *If you aren't sure about your abilities in your craft, ask trusted friends who know the business, and take independent, objective assessments.*

Skills

Are you good at your craft? This is another of those questions that require both honesty and discipline. You can be starting out. There's nothing wrong with that. On the other hand, if your skills are advanced, your plan for your business should reflect this too.

How do you assess your skills? This is an area where I can only provide general guidance, because it depends on your craft. If you are a photographer, the measures you use to determine your skill set will be very different from those of a painter. Likewise, a chef is different from a food stylist, and a singer is different from a songwriter.

You might notice that those examples are very close in the craft they practice. People look at the two-dimensional end result in the first example. In the second case, they both work with food, and creating with music is in the last example. That is intentional. Someone can be a great songwriter, but can't use more than three notes when they sing. Likewise, someone can create great flavor combinations, but arranging those on a plate in a manner that appeals to the public may not be their strong suit. The photographer uses a camera, and the painter, a brush.

How do you determine your level of skill? Your field guides this. Are formal assessment tools typically used to measure skills? Do informal means tell you where you fall on the creative spectrum? Can you ask others what they think? Do you have a loyal following? Does it matter, as long as your work sells?

Yes, I mentioned that concept so many creatives shy away from, money. I applaud those of you who create for the sake of creating! If you never intend to make your creative life into a revenue generator, that provides you with freedoms to do whatever you want. Good or bad, accepted or not, you are out there to have fun. That should be part of your plan! (Though in this case, I would say forget about writing a plan – you're out to have fun!)

For those of us who want to make money from our passion, I caution that money cannot be its own indicator. There are too many variables – subjective likes or dislikes of an audience, pricing strategies, and distribution channels to name a few. Being as financially successful as YOU want to be is the only bank balance you need to use in this part of the assessment.

STRENGTHS: What is your level of skill in your chosen creative field?

IMPROVEMENTS: What skills should you develop to continue to advance your improvements?

> *You can learn about your craft – but it's hard to teach passion.*

Education

Have you received formal education in your craft? In some fields, a degree is deemed a rite of passage. In others, it's not as important and can even be viewed as a creative detriment.

Some of you might say, "Why do I <u>need</u> an education? I'm creative – I produce what I feel like doing."

BUT...

If you plan to paint but have never used the tools before, not knowing how to use them will slow you down. If you want to take photos but don't know how to use the settings on your camera or frame a shot, your work may be good by accident – but accidents won't happen often!

No matter how much you already know, there are also always new things to learn. It may not be about your craft itself, but about the business around your craft. For example, the expectations readers have in specific fiction genres changes on an ongoing basis, so writers need to stay abreast of what those are so they satisfy their readers. The business side changes even faster, and in this case, continuous education is key.

STRENGTHS: What education have you had that serves to better your creative life?

IMPROVEMENTS: What else do you need to learn?

Set appointments with yourself for your major tasks of the day, but only AFTER you do your new creative work.

Lifestyle

How does your lifestyle support your creative life? Do you have a day job? Are you single, financially secure and free to work when you want, or do you have a busy family life that requires you to squeeze in creative time in small bites?

Do you have good support from your family and friends, or do they belittle your efforts?

Lifestyle does not need to be a barrier, even if there are aspects of it that do not support your creative time as much as you'd like. You can work around it. I won't go into the many suggestions about how to find creative minutes in your day. Sometimes, instead of fighting against boundaries, this is the opportunity to set some. Particularly if you are someone who does for everyone else in your life, claim some of that time back for yourself! Set an appointment for creative time, and stick to it!

If creativity is your full time job, are you using that time for the best results? Have you set time aside for each of the usual culprits in terms of time stealers? We can easily procrastinate by not setting time aside for pure creativity, versus running our creative business. I recommend setting appointments with yourself for your major tasks of the day, with creative time as the first priority. Protect that time at all costs! It's the first time slot you set and the one that is sacrosanct.

STRENGTHS: How does your lifestyle support your creative life?

IMPROVEMENTS: How can you set time in stone for your creative work?

> *No single group will meet all of your needs. Neither should you expect every benefit the group offers to be something you need.*

Connections

Sometimes, it IS who you know! Networking with others of similar or related interests allows us to leverage our skills, education and distribution in a synergistic manner. We help them succeed, and they (hopefully) return the favor. What are effective networking options? I classify them as formal (paid) membership associations, informal networks where voluntary participation is your 'fee', and loose contacts where you can offer each other something mutually beneficial.

Professional associations offer a number of benefits, from staying current on trends in your field to generating new ideas for your work. Whether it's an artists' cooperative or a writers' group, we can join together to make our single voice louder. I belong to a number of writer organizations, both formal and informal, and each bring me something different. The national organizations offer me education opportunities, industry information, and access to vendors and suppliers at a discount. Smaller informal groups give me brainstorming advice, local book signing events I would not have the draw to run as a single author, and commiserating friendship.

Loose contacts are a different animal. In this case, you might find someone who offers a complementary product or service to yours, and you get together to help each other out. Examples would include an art show at a fair, where you can show your work, while the show organizers benefit from having more wares to offer the public. An independent bookstore can encourage authors to come in for readings and signings, driving traffic to the store while giving the author exposure. A restaurant might be willing to allow a musician to play. Think about the unique linkages your work has and who might be have similar or aligning interests to your creative themes.

Two things to consider when you think about your connections are what you expect to get out of the joining, and curbing your expectations. What do you want out of the group? Education is different from one-on-one assistance. Political clout and advocacy in your craft field are best found in large formal membership organizations. Personalized assistance in exposing your work to a new audience might be more appropriate at a local level.

Now that you've set expectations, you need to be realistic about others! No single group will meet all of your needs. Neither should you expect every benefit the group offers to be something *you* need. It's a group, and by definition, it intends to offer something for everyone – but not everything will be appropriate for every member. If you do not need something the group offers but it will be a benefit for others, it's a good thing. Something for everyone!

STRENGTHS: What do you expect from networking opportunities? What connections do you have now through personal relationships, groups or associations?

IMPROVEMENTS: What gaps can you identify in your needs from connections? What connections do you need to cultivate to have those needs met?

It's form time again!

Craft Analysis

What am I good at, and how well do I know my craft?		
	OPPORTUNITIES	IMPROVEMENTS
Skills		
Education		
Lifestyle		
Connections		
Other		

> *When the world at large is crazy and people feel out of control, they need more of what we offer as creatives as a healthy means of escape.*

ENVIRONMENTAL ANALYSIS

The environment you work in is not only your personal space. Your art exists in a larger world. I truly believe that when the world at large is crazy and people feel out of control, they need more of what we offer as creatives as a healthy means of escape. You are on a mission to create a happier big world! Off my soapbox now...

The external environment we work in is outside of our control by definition. As such, I do not spend a lot of time focused on this part of this assessment. On the negative side, we can react to them. Reacting takes away what little control you DO have. You want to ACT on the realities of your external environment.

In other words, find the opportunities in your environment and capitalize on them. If something is a threat in terms of competition, market, or lifestyle, figure out how to minimize its impact on your creative life. There's nothing wrong with working *around a problem* instead of trying to solve it straight-out.

Examples of externalities you want to act upon include things like lack of access to distribution channels, lack of acceptance for your type of creative body of work in your community (however you define it), and lack of a voice about your field. Your plan can reflect what proactive measures you will take to overcome or work around the external factors that can block the business of your creative work.

Remember, having to commute for a long period each day is not an externality, because you can control the time in your day that is yours past working and commuting and family. Having no distribution channels available is an external factor because, unless you are willing to set them up, you need them to assist with your business. (Today, though, even this can be considered something you can control. We'll discuss this more in the marketing section.) No voice? Join an association – or form one.

Note: In this area, I have not suggested possible categories of things you should consider. I purposefully left out specifics because only you know what can hold you back or delay you. I don't want to put ideas in your head! Fill in the blanks as factors come to mind.

OPPORTUNITIES: What are the good things I cannot control that impact my creative life and I wish to take advantage of?

IMPROVEMENTS: What external factors outside of my direct control should I recognize as issues in the

successful implementation of my sustainable creative life? How will I take advantage of them or work around them?

Here's the place to recap the things you cannot control in the world around you (but can find a way to work to your advantage).

Environmental Analysis

FACTOR	IMPACT	ADVANTAGE
What are the things I cannot control that impact my creative life? How can I plan to take advantage of them or work around them? (add your own factors on the left)		

STEP 3 - WHAT DO I CREATE?

No matter what kind of creative work you produce, you require some idea of what your end product will be before you start. It can be as simple as saying it's a musical recording, or it's an original painting, or it's a book. It can also be as complex as the many formats for your work. You might have a different brand based on the product, so the way you represent yourself changes too.

In this section, we'll add the types of products you offer to your planning document. There are a number of ways to represent this. I have included examples here, but feel free to 'create' the system that works best for your style!

BRAND

There is no other creative like YOU in the world. We (the world) are lucky to have you! But who are YOU, exactly?

In terms of your creative life, that brand is the expectation you set with your audience about what you will provide. It's an informal contract with your audience about the experience they will enjoy. It's therefore very important you are clear about what image you want to portray.

A brand is not the same as a name, though it can be close, depending on the creative field you work in. For example, an author might be known by one name for bloody thriller books, and another for highbrowed literary fiction. Each name represents a brand setting up different expectations for the reader.

A musician, on the other hand, might work across different styles of music but keep the same name. In this case, the brand becomes harder to identify easily. How many of you have bought a playlist or album by a favorite artist, just to find they had changed styles and you don't like what they now do? The same might be the case for visual artists. You can see how the same name but different brand identity muddies the proverbial waters.

At the other end of the continuum, let's explore the food creative industry. A well-known chef opens a restaurant and is known for that particular cuisine. The place may or may not be named after the chef. The restaurant and its offerings – and maybe the chef – become an interlaced brand. But then they open a new place – different menu, different name, different feel. Does the chef's name tie into that brand too? If the expectation for the food is different, a name tie-in might confuse dining patrons.

Once you have determined your brand, you want to use it consistently when addressing your target audience. It's a name, but so much more. It's your viewpoint, your presence, and sometimes even the way you look. For example, there are artists who take strong political or advocacy positions – and others just as determined not to take any public position.

They dress a certain way that their audience expects, and may even act a certain why (outrageous or not). They may be committed to spreading word about their work through social media or a blog, or they may rely only on advertising and marketing, or they may do none of that.

Notations about the brand you use will be included in the product/service exercise we do next. For the time being, here are the important questions to ask yourself *for each brand you think you might have*:

What identifier/name am I using for this brand?

When do I use this brand?

What does the audience expect from this brand? (genre, category, image)

What brand materials do I need for this audience? (physical, online such as website or blog or social media, presence)

An example of how I completed the brand form is included on the following page.

EXAMPLE OF ONE OF MY BRANDS

Name/Identifier for BRAND Goose Your Muse – writing as Y K Kohano (link to Yvonne Kohano in materials)
Audience Expectations for BRAND Tips to help creative people be more creative – written from the authors point of view, but incorporating examples from other mediums and genres
BRAND Use For nonfiction products. Also cross-sell with romantic suspense and with psychological thrillers/thrillers.
BRAND Materials Website: www.GooseYourMuse.com Facebook: Goose Your Muse Twitter: @GooseYourMuse Blog with tips for creatives at website. ***Tagline:*** "Tips for Creatives"; "Building Blocks to be Your Best Creative Self" Media kit specific to the brand. Cross-sell with Yvonne Kohano and Y J Kohano, Kohano website. Unique business cards. Brand image – color graphic covers against white background

Audience

We already talked about the expectations of your audience based on your brand. But who is that audience? What do you know about them? The better you can draw conclusions about their general characteristics, the better job you can do of creating a message that reaches them.

You might be concerned that we're painting individuals with too broad a brush here. Don't be. Categories are our way of organizing a complex, messy world. When you make assumptions about your audience, there will obviously be outliers who don't fit into the category. You are trying to identify the vast majority – and hoping they tell everyone else.

Where do you find this category information? This gets tricky, because sometimes it's obvious in your creative field, and sometimes you need to dig deep. It might be based on a type of medium, or a grouping of products, or individual items. This is an "it depends" situation where you need to use your creative muscle to figure out what makes your audience unique, and also uniquely able to like YOU.

One more caution on audiences. Be careful about drawing too narrow an audience band. For example, if you believe your work will *only* appeal to a small group of people, you run into two problems. First, how will you reach everyone in this very specialized group? Secondly, will they be able to buy enough of what you're selling to support your goals? Niche can be a blessing – and a curse.

Ready to think about your audience? Formulate your answer to the following question:

For** (pick your product by category or item**), my audience will be...

Distribution Channels

There are three ways to handle your documentation of your distribution channels. One is to organize this by brand, in which case you will want to do this exercise after you create the brand categorization. The next is to do this by product line, which means you'd do it as part of your product line assessment in the previous step. Or, you do it by item. The method you select needs to make sense to you, based on the creative products you offer.

Some final thoughts on distribution. Depending on your level of technical capability, some channels might be more difficult for you to access than others. For example, you can take a photo, but can you convert it into a poster? How about selling it on stock photo websites? Or turning it into framed pictures? You can handle some of these things yourself, but in other cases, you might have to hire someone to help you. DO NOT feel compelled to try every possible channel from your first days as a creative. Do what works for you, and add more later as your ability, bank account and nerves allow.

Time to answer the next question:

For *(*pick your product by category or item*), **my methods of distribution will be...**

Now it's your turn!

Brand (complete one page for each brand you have)

Name/Identifier for BRAND
Audience Expectations for BRAND
BRAND Use
BRAND Materials

PRODUCTS

As a creative, it is sometimes difficult to think about our precious creation as a *product*. It is, after all, **art**. But even art falls into categories and classifications, and there are many ways to reach what could be a diverse rich audience. Here's an example.

I write a book. I can then release it in ebook, paper, and audio versions. I can have different sizes of paperback. I can distribute the ebook (or any of the other formats) through various distribution channels. I might change the cover or the description based on the audience I want to reach. Pricing will vary based on format and may also vary based on channel within the same format.

As you can imagine, the number of variations grow exponentially with each new opportunity in an industry. Think of the many ways someone can now distribute their music! Or post photos or videos, for free or for sale. Or how many different forms a piece of physical art like a painting can now be represented. The ways you can expose your creative product to the world are often only limited by your time. (I won't say imagination. You have that – you're a creative!)

Here's a sample of the kinds of decisions you can make about something as simple as these Goose Your Muse books.

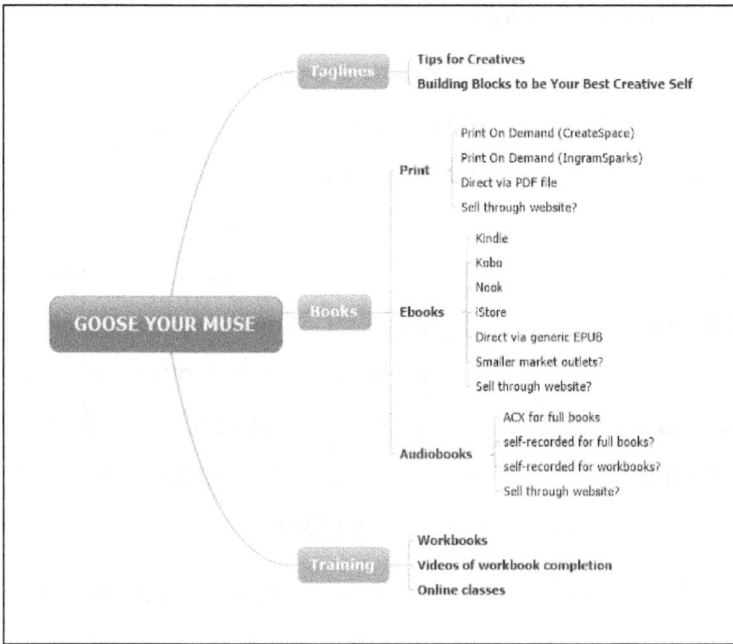

GOOSE YOUR MUSE

Taglines
- Tips for Creatives
- Building Blocks to be Your Best Creative Self

Books

Print
- Print On Demand (CreateSpace)
- Print On Demand (IngramSparks)
- Direct via PDF file
- Sell through website?

Ebooks
- Kindle
- Kobo
- Nook
- iStore
- Direct via generic EPUB
- Smaller market outlets?
- Sell through website?

Audiobooks
- ACX for full books
- self-recorded for full books?
- self-recorded for workbooks?
- Sell through website?

Training
- Workbooks
- Videos of workbook completion
- Online classes

Let's make this even more complicated. This is just *one of my product lines!* I also have a romantic suspense series, and a psychological thriller series. Each appeals to a different audience, and the brands for each are different too. Clearly, this can create many combinations and permutations.

You DO NOT need to make it complicated. Figure out what makes sense for your work, the general ways that you want to classify it, and how you want to break into categories. Start simple, and as your creative business becomes more sophisticated, you can add more branches, pages or worksheets.

Current Products

Think about your products as inventory. Even something as unique and specific as an oil painting can have multiple uses. You can sell the painting itself, but that's one time think. How about making glycee prints of it and issuing those in a limited edition run? Card stock or posters, anyone? Electronic use as a background for a motivation poster or release for photo stock use are other opportunities. This is how you leverage your work! You created the original oil painting once, but it can keep on contributing long after that first sale if you have other formats for it.

You might be thinking, "Yes, Yvonne, for something tangible and long-lasting, that might work, but what about food artists?" True, the chef creates a meal, it is consumed, and that representation is gone. But how about cookbooks, or an online cooking video channel, or live demonstrations? The chef creates the recipe once, but it can keep on giving too.

I'll be the first person to tell you that creating your product grid can be incredibly tedious if you already have a large body of work. For the time being, you don't need to work this down to the per-unit item basis (like a single work of physical art or book) unless you really want to – or have a short list of units to work with. Try working by category, and capturing where you are now and where you want to go.

Here are some examples. As with anything in this book, go to the level of detail and formatting that makes the most sense for you. Mine have evolved over the years as I have identified a need for greater detail or additional tracking. Design a system that works for you!

Example: Audience Analysis by Product Line

Product Line	*Audience Characteristics*
Goose Your Muse	Creative people in various genres and mediums – writers, artists, photographers, musicians – who need help planning for the growth of their business
Flynn's Crossing	Romance readers who like suspense in their small town stories. 89% female, age 25+. Listing of similar author likes.
Mind Web	Thriller readers who favor psychological themes. Not gender specific, not age specific. Listing of similar author likes.

Example: Product information formatted as a spreadsheet (metadata)

NONFICTION METADATA	Release Date	ISBN - ebook	ISBN - paper	Copyright Filed	Ebook Price	Paper Price
Goose Your Muse						
Business Planning	09/06/16	978-1-940XXX-XX-X	978-1-940XXX-XX-X	09/06/16	X.99	X.99
More Creative You	09/13/16	978-1-940XXX-XX-X	978-1-940XXX-XX-X	09/13/16	X.99	X.99

Example: Product formatted as description (partial listing)

Title: FOUR STEPS TO BUSINESS PLANNING FOR THE PLAN-PHOBIC CREATIVE
Subtitle: Goose Your Muse Tips for Creatives Series
w/a: Y J Kohano

Long Description:

Planning inhibits your sense of creative flow. It takes up too much time. Besides, what would you put in a plan? Or you're at the other end of continuum. You absolutely *love* to plan. Your to-do list is your bible, and you study it every day. Checking things off that list is an obsession for you. Give you a color-coding system and you are over the proverbial moon. Or you're in the middle, that place where you know you *should* plan, but you're not sure *why*. People tell you it's important to grow your creative life, but, like our friends in no-plan land, you wouldn't know where to start.

No matter where you fall in the continuum of planning for your creative life, you can make things easier, simpler, and faster by designing the right kind of business plan. I'm not talking about the whole mission-vision-values-goals-objectives-tactics and documentation that would make even the most organized person's head spin. We want things focused, direct and supportive. *FOUR STEPS TO BUSINESS PLANNING FOR THE PLAN-PHOBIC CREATIVE* gives you a useful tool to guide your best creative life.

Release: Sept 2016

About the GOOSE YOUR MUSE Tips for Creatives Series: Building blocks for your best creative self! Being creative can be the ultimate joy – or a disappointing challenge. What if you could eliminate the painful parts, like running the business side or running out of ideas? This series is designed for creatives types in any field, with advice on keeping the fun in our daily creatives lives.

Keywords: Kindle
creativity, creative, business planning, artist, writer, small business, entrepreneur

Categories: Kindle
Nonfiction > SELF-HELP > Creativity
Nonfiction > BUSINESS & ECONOMICS > Small Business

Keywords: CreateSpace
creativity, creative, business planning, small business, entrepreneur

Categories: CreateSpace
SELF-HELP > Creativity

Future Products

Now that you have a handle on your brands and your existing products, it's time to think about your future body of creative work. Important factors you will now be adding to your format include what you plan to work on next. This can be as specific as a concept of the work, or as vague as "three more in the series". The frequency of completion/release, and perhaps if it's in progress already, some estimate of how far along you are or how far you have yet to go can also be included. A time budget to complete the work is also often useful. Add these to the format that works best for you.

There are other things you might want to add to YOUR product listing. As a writer, I might want to include keywords I use to describe each book for various distribution channels. A physical artist might include the period name of that work, like the "blue period". A photographer might want the inspirational location listed. It's YOUR listing. Add or delete based on what makes the most sense for you.

You now have examples of how you want to plan for the products you offer and their future use. Use color if that works for you. Make this a text explanation if that's a better method in your style. Or take pictures. It's up to you! Work on this for a time, and after you make some headway, return to the next section to visit your audience in more depth.

Current Products (complete one for each existing product/product line)

Product:
Description:
Keywords/Identifiers/Descriptors:
Audience Characteristics:
Distribution Channels:
Pricing Strategy:

Future Product Planning (complete one for each anticipated product/product line)

Product:
Description:
Anticipated Production Period and Hours of Effort:
Key Deadlines: (advanced marketing and promotion, outside edits and reviews, etc.)
Anticipated Release Date:
Promotional Strategy:

STEP 4 – HOW WILL I ALLOCATE MY RESOURCES?

Any creative business includes non-creative tasks. You know the ones, the things you really *don't* like to do. There is a trade-off: you can create, or you can manage. In addition to what you can afford to spend in dollars, you must think about where you want to expend effort.

For example, this book includes a variety of spreadsheets, graphics, and inserts. While I can easily format and upload the file for a paper version, the special requirements of these many types of examples mean a more sophisticated software program must be used to generate the file acceptable for ebook production.

I love learning new things! I get a kick out of figuring out how things work. A new formatting program sounds like fun to me. BUT…

Do I have the time to learn a new program, while completing the necessary editing and review tasks associated with a new release? Can I simultaneously manage the beta reader process AND implement the marketing plan for this book, while tackling the necessary (but steep) learning curve for a complex new program? Is this even the best use of my time, longer term?

This comes down to a make-versus-buy decision. Usually, if the new skill (the software program) is something I believe I'll use frequently, I'll invest the time to learn what I need to do so that I can do it myself. BUT...

My time is limited.

My deadline is SOON!

My upcoming releases will not require me to be using this software frequently.

In this case, I'll "buy" the use of someone else's time to prepare the final formatted manuscript for me. It makes more sense for me to invest my limited resources (time) in the next books. The same thought process can apply to everything from accounting to delivery of supplies.

The question you need to answer is: ***What commodity is unique to you? Simple – the creation of the "thing".*** Creative time is always your first priority.

After that, what commodity is in the *shortest supply* for you? That will be the next filter for your decision-making. Sometimes more than one commodity is on a tight budget, in which case you need to decide which is more important for you, both immediately and in the longer term.

Time as Currency
By now, you have raised quite a few considerations about the time you want or need to invest in your creative

business. Time is currency. It is a limited commodity and you have to spend it wisely. Multiple factors should be considered here.

The first factor is time to create. Be realistic here. None of us, no matter how talented, can create nonstop for unending periods of time. Not you. Certainly not me! I work in creative spurts, sometimes only two hours long before I need a break (though I have been known to go on a creative bender and write for ten hours in a day).

Not everyone can live their creative life as a full time business, either. Day jobs are necessary to pay the bills, or some offshoot of our creative life (like offering a creative service to others to help fill their gaps) may be necessary.

Identify the time you have available to devote to the creative life. Do not say "all of my time", even if your creative life is your full time job. It is still a job – it is not the only thing you will do in your waking hours.

Break the time up into actionable energy steps. Some of us are better at 'new work' when we're fresh in the morning, and others might prefer late at night. When do you have the best energy for each kind of activity?

Assign time to each function – new creation, editing or reworking drafted projects, administrative work, marketing, etc. Do it in a way that is meaningful for you. I start with a month, then break that into weekly accomplishments at the beginning of each month, then daily at the beginning of each week.

BE REALISTIC!

Here's a sample of the kind of worksheet I would use as I started out.

Example: Creative Time Checklist

Activity/Frequency	*Planning*
PRIORITY 1: New work creation – 3 hours a day	Make an appointment on my calendar to block that creative time
PRIORITY 2: Editing existing works in process – 2 hours a day	Make an appointment on my calendar *after new work creative time is completed*
Exercise – 1 hour a day	Appointment!
Marketing & promotion – 1 hour a day	Appointment!
Education – take 1 online class per month	Review online listings to identify appropriate classes – midmonth for following month. Make an appointment in my calendar for class time as needed.
Review/implement 1 new technology asset per month	Sources: various. Identify and set time aside as calendar allows.

Your turn!

Activity/Frequency	*Planning*
PRIORITY 1:	
PRIORITY 2:	

Control

What do you give up when you move a service or product outside? Control. I don't know about you but I'm a control freak! Giving it up to someone else means I have to plan more time to allow them to complete their work than I would need myself. Let's face it, they have busy professional lives too. Scheduling may become an issue. I have to complete my steps earlier in the timeline to offer them enough time to get their job done. Similarly, there is an investment I would need to make in managing the services or contractors I hire.

One final point that's important to make is the need to hire one particular kind of service in your field, and that's objective review of your work. If you're a writer, you've heard the caution that you should never be your own editor. Musicians may think the song is great, but could they hear a problem while they're rehearsing a song? As creatives, we may "know" something isn't right, but to determine exactly what that is, we need another set of eyes on a project. Hire help for this, and don't even blink at the cost.

Hiring Out

As long as we're on the subject of hiring out the work, let's discuss what other planning considerations you should have when you hire out some of your non-creative workload.

Time should be spent on finding the 'right' person for you. Look at examples of their work. Ask for references, and check them. Confirm their reliability in both quality of the work and meeting deadlines. Price-shop among your choices – though lowest cost does not necessarily equate to best outcome for you.

Consider too the amount of your time required when using anyone on the outside. Even your accountant needs you to pull receipts together. You will need to plan for time to do the necessary raw data collection work – or raw editing, or initial reviews of your songs, or thinking about distribution channels for your photos or physical art. You are the chief executive officer of your creative business, and that means the big picture decisions about future directions as well as operations belong to you. Hire to fill in the gaps you do not want to fill yourself.

Make or buy. You decide. Here are some things to think about in preparation for completing your skills gaps worksheet.

What skill or process gaps do you have in your overall business?

Which gaps would you be willing to fill in yourself? What do you need to do to prepare for this?

Who can you hire to fill in the remaining gaps?

What due diligence will you need to perform to confirm you are selecting the right person?

How does the time investment for managing the outside assistance fit with the rest of your creative business?

Ready to fill in the gaps?

Skill Gap	Investment Required (time or money)

Structure and Protection

I cannot advise you on your specific legal and financial structure. This is a discussion you need to have with trusted local professionals, as the laws and regulations related to both areas differ by state and sometimes city. This is one of those oversight opportunities where is pays to invest in expert help. Many large cities have a resource center for small businesses, and advisory services are available on a free or low-fee basis. Many tax accountants and small business attorneys also offer a free hour of discussion on your specific circumstances.

That being said, here are factors to consider as you prepare for your professional discussions. The rule of thumb is to calculate how much risk you are willing to assume. The risk ALWAYS has a financial component. Here are some examples.

We talked before about creative risk. Business risk is different. Could someone sue you? Even if they would not win in the long run, if there is a reasonable chance a judge would accept the case, you will need to pay to defend yourself. The greater this kind of risk, the more you want to distance your creative business in a legal and financial sense from your personal life.

You might think this will never apply to you. But, let's say you *inadvertently* violate the law by using a logo in a piece of art. Or your model is injured on a photo shoot. Or someone says you plagiarized their music or words. They can sue you. Even if they do not win, you need to pay an attorney to handle your case up front. (Yes, the obvious answer is to never get into this situation, but in our excitement to create, we are sometimes naïve and make an honest mistake.)

Another major reason to set up a separate legal and financial structure is the tax man. The good old IRS loves commerce, and applauds your success because that means you'll be paying taxes at some point. (You WILL be successful, right?) The five-year rule says you can generate losses at the beginning of a business's life, but to continue to deduct those losses as a tax write-off, you need to show progress in your business – and get to a breakeven point in five years.

There may be exceptions, and one of those is being able to prove you have an ongoing business concern. A planning document such as you are creating here is one such item of proof! Even if you do not create a separate legal structure for your business, you are thinking about it like a professional business person.

Another is financial documentation proving you are reinvesting everything you make from your business in further growing the business. Some creative types are really good at staying organized for the business side of their creative work. They log their expenses and revenues into an accounting program or on a spreadsheet. They are comfortable doing their own taxes at the end of the year. Others forget to get receipts. Or if they do get them, they throw them in a shoebox – maybe. Taxes, schmaxes. On April 15, they're frantically searching for the shoebox. These shoeboxers might need a bookkeeping service in addition to a tax accountant.

What kinds of risks might I be open to as a result of my creative work?

What kinds of contractual relationships might I have?

What skills do I have for the financial end of the business?

Who can I consult for additional information?

Succession Planning

Few among us like to dwell on the fact that we won't be here forever, but it's the one thing guaranteed for all of us. What happens to your body of creative work when you're no longer around? It outlives you, but someone needs to control it and someone needs to manage it. Make no assumptions about your heirs being willing, knowledgeable or capable of handling sales or distribution without specific instructions. Families are torn apart when they don't agree on next steps at a time when they are emotionally fragile.

This is where the help of a good family law attorney with intellectual property experience is key. You may be the creator of a piece of work, but you may not own the rights to it just because you create it.

Examples are endless. On a very simple level, a painting is sold, and the buyer has rights to it – not the artist. An author writes a book, but the publisher who releases that book owns the rights to it, and that publisher controls the rights until either the contract period is up (rights revert to the author or the author's estate) or 70 years after the death of the author (copyright law).

But then what happens? Who gets the body of work where the rights still reside with the creator? What about unfinished works? What can be sold, and under what conditions? How are revenues from those sales then distributed? It all comes down to control, and a thoughtful creative will make plans for the future when they are no longer around to be the control freak!

Considerations here are also based on the laws in your state, and the type of legal planning you want to prepare for your estate. It is part of your personal estate planning. Ergo, legal help required!

What do I want done with my completed works for which I have the rights after my death?

What about unfinished works? Can someone else complete them? Should they be destroyed?

Check out the final worksheet on the following page!

Hiring Professionals

Professional Need	Questions I Have & Planning
Business Risks	
Legal Structure	
Accounting Services	
Succession Planning	

WHAT HAPPENS NEXT?

Time to review everything you've done – and you've done a lot! Let's pull their pieces together.

The following section contains blank worksheets for you to complete or modify – as you wish! They are also available in an editable text format at my website, www.GooseYourMuse.com. Stop by, download the set, and modify them as you wish.

Your plan is only as good as your commitment to it. This is a dynamic process, not a static document you put on the shelf and ignore until something "happens". Make this a part of your regular planning. When you finish a new body of work, update the plan for the next big thing on your horizon.

Now is a good time to also think about how you want to measure your progress against the targets and actions you planned throughout this book. Monthly? Quarterly? Once a year? To begin with, monthly is good, just so you remind yourself what tasks you want to take on in the coming period. After that, it's as often as you need reminders – and want to make course adjustments to your commitments.

Commitment also means accountability to others, so share your plan. Do you have creative partners, like a critique or brainstorming group? Get them on board with what you plan to achieve and report back regularly. Let them keep you honest about working toward your goals! And return the favor! (Sometimes it's fun to each develop a creative plan and work toward your goals together, then reward the group on their good achievements with a special celebration. Anything to stay motivated!)

I hope **FOUR STEPS TO BUSINESS PLANNING FOR THE PLAN-PHOBIC CREATIVE** has met my goal, offering you a useful tool to guide *your best creative life*. That's the most important thing to remember if you only take away one after this time we've spent together. This is a *tool*, one that will *work for you if you let it*. Try out the methods outlined here, and let me know how your future unfolds in **YOUR BEST CREATIVE LIFE!**

MY BEST CREATIVE LIFE WORKBOOK

STEP 1 – What's My Purpose?

What do I want?

In my best creative life, I want...

Why do I want it?

I want to be a creative because...	
Important Factors:	
Art	
Passion	
Money	
Lifestyle	
Career	
Other	

Notes to Me:

What do I value?

The values that guide my creative life are...	
Important Factors:	
Belief Systems	
Satisfaction First	
Internal Struggles	
Imposter Syndrome	
Comfort with Risk	
Other	

Notes to Me:

What does success look like?

I will be satisfied in my best creative life when...

Notes to Me:

STEP 2 – Who Am I?

Personal Inventory

How have my experiences prepared me for the creative life I want to explore?		
	STRENGTHS	**IMPROVEMENTS**
Life Skills		
Resources		
Perspective		
Work Habits		
Other		

Notes to Me:

Craft Analysis

What am I good at, and how well do I know my craft?		
	STRENGTHS	**IMPROVEMENTS**
Skills		
Education		
Lifestyle		
Connections		
Other		

Notes to Me:

Environmental Analysis

What are the things I cannot control that impact my creative life? How can I plan to overcome or work around them? (add your own factors on the left)		
	STRENGTHS	IMPROVEMENTS

Notes to Me:

Step 3 – What Do I Create?

Brand (complete one page for each brand you have)

Name/Identifier for BRAND
Audience Expectations for BRAND
BRAND Use
BRAND Materials

Notes to Me:

Current Products (complete one for each existing product/product line)

Product:
Description:
Keywords/Identifiers/Descriptors:
Audience Characteristics:
Distribution Channels:
Pricing Strategy:

Notes to Me:

Future Product Planning (complete one for each anticipated product/product line)

Product:
Description:
Anticipated Production Period and Hours of Effort:
Key Deadlines: *(advanced marketing and promotion, outside edits and reviews, etc.)*
Anticipated Release Date:
Promotional Strategy:

Notes to Me:

Step 4 – How Will I Allocate My Resources?

Creative Time Checklist

Activity/Frequency	Planning
PRIORITY 1:	
PRIORITY 2:	

Business Skill Gaps

Skill Gap	Investment Required (time or money)

Hiring Professionals

Professional Need	Questions I Have & Planning
Business Risks	
Legal Structure	
Accounting Services	
Succession Planning	

Also by Y J Kohano/Yvonne Kohano

GOOSE YOUR MUSE

Four Steps to Being a More Creative You

Four Steps to Business Planning for Plan-Phobic Creatives

Four Steps to Building Your Creative Market

MIND WEB PSYCHOLOGICAL THRILLER SERIES

Mind Stalked, Book 1

Mind Etched, Book 2

Mind Tangled, Book 3

FLYNN'S CROSSING ROMANTIC SUSPENSE SERIES

Pictures of Redemption, Book 1

Flashes of Fire, Book 2

Naked Intolerances, Book 3

Tastes and Consequences, Book 4

Blooms on the Bones, Book 5

Wine Into Water, Book 6

Love and the Christmas Tree Nymph, A Flynn's Crossing
Seasonal Novella

Love's Touch of Justice, Book 7

This Proposal Between Us, A Flynn's Crossing Seasonal
Novella

Measure Twice, Love Once, Book 8

Love's Fiery Prescription, Book 9

Love's Fiery Resolution, Book 10

And more to come!

Learn about upcoming releases at www.YvonneKohano.com.

Please leave an honest review of this nonfiction work at your favorite book discovery site of choice. I love to hear from readers, so feel free to contact me directly on Facebook as Yvonne Kohano, on Twitter @yvonnekohano, and at yvonne@yvonnekohano.com.

About the Author

Award winning storycatcher Y J Kohano/Yvonne Kohano writes contemporary romantic suspense, psychological thrillers, and nonfiction tips on creativity, when she's not gardening, cooking, traveling, reading or learning something new. Follow her at www.YvonneKohano.com (psychological thriller and romantic suspense fiction), www.GooseYourMuse.com (creativity tips), and Facebook and Twitter to learn what tickles her about being a writer.

www.ingramcontent.com/pod-product-compliance
Lightning Source LLC
Chambersburg PA
CBHW061754020426
42331CB00006B/1475